NATIONAL LAMPOON®

PRESENTS

MORE
TRUE FACTS

NATIONAL LAMPOON®

PRESENTS

MORE TRUE FACTS

An All-New Collection of Absurd-but-True
Real-Life Funny Stuff

COMPILED BY JOHN BENDEL

CB

CONTEMPORARY
BOOKS

CHICAGO

Library of Congress Cataloging-in-Publication Data

    National lampoon presents more true facts /
compiled by John Bendel.
      p.   cm.
   ISBN 0-8092-3942-6
   1. American wit and humor, Pictorial.   I. Bendel,
John.   II. National lampoon.   III. Title: More true facts.
NC1428.N374   1992
031.02—dc20

                                           91-39593
                                            CIP

Front cover photo contributed by Damon Foster.
Back cover photos contributed by Don Liverani
(left) and Jack Dakin (right); headline contributed by
Eric Ambro.

Published by Contemporary Books, Inc.
180 North Michigan Avenue, Chicago, Illinois 60601
Manufactured in the United States of America
International Standard Book Number: 0-8092-3942-6

To
The Commandant, Berner, Gubble, and da Kak

Report from the Editor

Welcome to *National Lampoon Presents More True Facts*, our second all-star collection of stories, headlines, signs, ads, photos, business cards, and, well, you name it, submitted by the readers of *National Lampoon* to a long-standing feature we call "True Facts."

True Facts? you may be wondering. Do you mean to say there are any other kinds of facts?

But of course, faithful reader. There are sordid facts, secondhand facts, unvarnished facts, salient facts, the facts of life, just the facts . . . in fact, there are more facts than any of us might ever have imagined. Hence, it is critical to distinguish between True Facts and other, more prevalent, less intriguing, and yes, quite frankly, inferior facts. The following quiz should illuminate the essential differences.

Q. Which is the True Fact?
- **A.** According to the *Information Please Almanac*, Sir H. Campbell-Bannerman served as prime minister of Britain from 1905 to 1908.
- **B.** According to the *Gannett Reporter Dispatcher*, a White Plains, New York, youth was charged with indecent exposure after he allegedly dropped his pants in front of a person dressed as Gumby.

Q. Which is the True Fact?
- **A.** A headline from a recent edition of the *New York Times* proclaimed "Dollar Off Again Against the Yen."
- **B.** A headline from the *Fitchburg Sentinel and Enterprise* proclaimed "Colon Outburst Highlights Trial."

In both examples, item B was, in fact, the True Fact. I'm sure you'll agree with us that each outclassed its mundane competitor, clearly demonstrating the superiority of True Facts over lesser sorts of data.

Please note that the above quiz was meant for *educational purposes only.* Official True Fact classification should always be left to highly trained specialists. That would be us.

Which brings us to the point: If you have an item you believe might be a True Fact—whether it's something you've clipped or copied or photographed—please send that potential True Fact for analysis to:

True Facts
National Lampoon
155 Avenue of the Americas
New York, NY 10013

(That's what Jeff Reed, who submitted the Gumby True Fact, and Bruce Siart, who submitted the Colon True Fact, did—and *now their names are in print*.)

Experts will subject your submission to technical evaluation under highly controlled conditions and come to a determination. If tests prove positive, you'll be sent a True Facts T-shirt and *your name* will accompany your True Fact upon publication, forever placing you in the bright and shining light of True Facts glory.

Thank you.

You may read the rest of the book now.

John Bendel

Miss Brenda Sue Powers

Local man engaged

From the *Worthington* (Ohio) *News*;
contributed by Alan Brady

Corn Country Excitement

Iowans in uproar over Chinese hog semen

From the *Cedar Rapids Gazette*;
contributed by Bill Irwin

Photo contributed by Daniel Santolini

Just park and wait your turn, pal.

Photo contributed by Jim Wright

A NATURAL CHOICE

"I'm happy! I've got gas!"
– Dave Hunter

From the *Vincennes* (Indiana) *Sun-Commercial*; contributed by Judy Eaton

Earphones for minnows

Photo contributed by Jim Kavalier

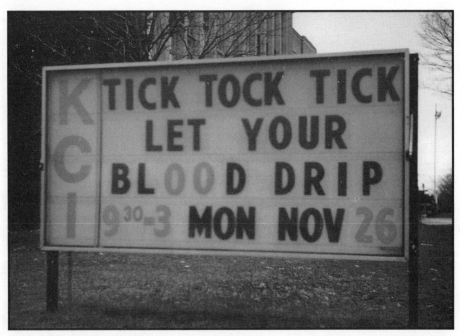

Photo contributed by David G. Lynn

Featuring light snacks from hell's kitchen

Photo contributed by Don M. Miller

Home of the Well-Done Burger

HELLBURGER
Your Gyros Speciality Restaurant

Dönerkebab (Gyros) Sandwich	DM 5.—	Fishburger	DM 3.50
Hellburger	DM 2.—	Schnitzel with Pommes Frites	DM 5.70
Cheeseburger	DM 2.20	Chickenfilet	DM 4.20
Doppeldecker	DM 4.50	Chicken Chips	DM 4.20
Big Burger	DM 4.—	Pommes Frites small	DM 1.50
Jumbo	DM 5.20	Pommes Frites big	DM 2.—
Ham und Cheese	DM 3.20	Potato-salad	DM 1.50
Schnitzelsandwich	DM 5.—	Coleslaw	DM 1.50

Opening Times:
Sunday - Thurs: 11⁰⁰a.m. - 1⁰⁰a.m.
Friday - Sat: 11⁰⁰a.m. - 4⁰⁰a.m.

Dollars accepted
Wuerzburger Str. 102
8750 Aschaffenburg
Phone 0 60 21-9 15 34

From a West German newspaper; contributed by Eric Damm

Only two blocks from Middle of the Road

Photo contributed by Dan Sevsek

Photo contributed by Randy Wood

Subliminal Substances

▼ ▼ ▼ ▼ ▼ ▼ ▼ ▼ ▼ ▼

Photo contributed
by Michelle Hansen

Photo contributed by Avery Frost

Photo contributed by Jack Dakin

Toward Increased Global Warming

HOW WOMEN'S TOP 25 FARTED

How the Associated Press' Top 25 women's teams fared this week:

- 1. Virginia (27-2) did not play. beat North Carolina 90-69; lost to Clemson 65-62.
- 2. Penn State (26-1) did not play. beat No. 24 George Washington 77-62. beat St. Joseph's 76-40.
- 3. Georgia (26-3) did not play. beat South Alabama 125-64; beat Alabama 78-69. lost to No. 12 LSU 83-74.
- 4. Tennessee (25-4) did not play. beat Vanderbilt 62-60; beat No. 5 Auburn 70-62.
- 5. Auburn (24-5) did not play. beat No. 18 Mississippi 76-50. lost to No. 4 Tennessee 70-62.
- 6. Purdue (24-2) did not play. beat Illinois 112-49.
- 7. North Carolina State (25-5) did not play. beat E. Carolina 116-73. beat Wake Forest 92-72. beat Maryland 82-75.
- 8. Arkansas (24-3) did not play. beat Baylor 90-74.
- 9. Washington (21-4) beat UCLA 64-54.
- 10. Stanford (22-4) did not play. beat California 93-80;
- 11. Western Kentucky (25-2) did not play. beat Old Dominion 73-63; beat Virginia Commonwealth 102-84.
- 12. LSU (23-6) did not play. beat No. 19 Stephen F. Austin 79-77. beat Kentucky 96-76; beat No. 3 Georgia 83-74.
- 13. Connecticut (25-4) did not play. beat Pittsburgh 79-55; beat Villanova 64-47; beat Seton Hall 69-54.
- 14. Texas (20-7) did not play. beat Texas Tech 77-53. beat Texas Christian 77-40. beat Southern Methodist 90-52.
- 15. UNLV (24-5) did not play. beat Fresno State 72-69; beat Pacific 102-76.
- 16. Providence (25-4) did not play. beat Villanova 74-69. beat Georgetown 95-91; beat Pittsburgh 107-92.
- 17. Rutgers (22-5) did not play. beat St. Joseph's 73-51. lost to West Virginia 89-78.
- 18. Mississippi (20-8) did not play. beat Mississippi State 74-56. lost to No. 5 Auburn, 76-50.
- 19. Stephen F. Austin (23-4) did not play. lost to No. 12 LSU 79-77. beat McNeese State 101-41.
- 20. Northwestern (19-7) did not play. beat Indiana 87-71; beat Ohio State 71-55.
- 21. Iowa (18-8) did not play. beat Louisiana Tech 72-57. beat Michigan 76-64. lost to Michigan State 49-48.
- 22. Notre Dame (21-6) did not play. lost to Dayton 79-76. beat Xavier-Ohio 69-53.
- 23. Long Beach State (19-7) did not play. beat Pacific 91-73. beat San Jose State, 73-53.
- 24. George Washington (22-5) did not play. lost to No. 2 Penn State 77-62. beat St. Bonaventure, 84-59.
- 25. Lamar (25-2) did not play.

From the *Boulder* (Colorado) *Daily Camera*; contributed by Alan Hlava

Wit or windstorm?

Photo contributed by Tom Gallagher

Fish Rubs

Photo contributed by Joan C. Serivani

Two Feet and Digging

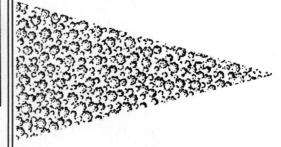

Frost-Line

Jeri-Lyn Frost and Donald Wayne Line, both of Indianapolis, were married March 9 in Bethany Lutheran Church.

Their parents are Mr. and Mrs. Gerald W. Frost, Mrs. Gary T. Leathers and Verle D. Line, all of Indianapolis. The couple graduated from Indiana University. The bride is a member of Alpha Chi Omega. She is a registered nurse in pediatric intensive care at Riley Hospital for Children. Her husband is a member of Chi Phi. He is owner of Beverage Enterprises Inc.

From the *Indianapolis Star*; contributed by Lucille Parr

Home of the Jiggle Shows

Photo contributed by Mary Nell Drust

Gee, Dad's tastes just like that bottled junk.

From *Parenting* magazine; contributed by Scott A. Edwards

. . . but do they float?

Photo contributed by Diana Schwabe

Pissing policeman loses handgun to 2 holdupmen

Two unidentified men reportedly armed with a handgun and a fan knife took the service revolver of a Quezon City policeman who was urinating in a vacant lot near a shopping mall in Mandaluyong Wednesday night.

The policeman was identified as Pat. Chito Aquino, 38, detailed with Station 4 of the Central Police District, of 1930 Mount Apo st., Punta, Sta. Ana, Manila.

Aquino told Mandaluyong police probers that the robbery happened at around 11:20 p.m. in a vacant lot between the EDSA Central mall and the Melvin department store.

Police said Aquino, who had been drinking that night, did not notice the two suspects approach as he was urinating.

Aquino lost only his Smith and Wesson .38 cal. revolver to the two unidentified men, who fled towards Shaw blvd. after the robbery. **(Jun Burgos)**

From the *Manila* (Philippines) *Standard*; contributed by Christopher Landrum

No smoking, please. Our last dog disappeared when someone lit up.

Photo contributed by Kimberly Montoya

Fowler-Colon

Susan Michelle Fowler of Odessa and Gregory Lawrence Colon of El Paso were married April 20 at Odessa Tabernacle Church with the Rev. Sam Jordon officiating.

The bride is the daughter of Mr. and Mrs. Johnny E. Fowler of Odessa. She is a 1983 graduate of Permian High School and a 1988 graduate of Texas Tech University with a degree in marketing. She is employed by Roadway Express in El Paso.

The groom is the son of Mr. and Mrs. Willard Linebert of Louisville, Ky., and the late Malcolm Colon. He is a 1983 graduate of Lewisville High School in Lewisville, a 1987 graduate of the University of Texas at Austin with a degree in finance and is a 1991 graduate of Texas Tech School of Medicine in Lubbock.

Mr. and Mrs. Gregory Lawrence Colon

From the *Odessa* (Texas) *American*; contributed by Michael L. Schuff

Ryan gets OK to kill religious school boards

SARAH SCOTT
THE GAZETTE

Education Minister Claude Ryan received legal backing from Quebec's highest court yesterday to abolish most Protestant and Catholic school boards and replace them with French and English boards.

From the *Montreal Gazette*; contributed by Bob Fiocco

Headless hollow, guaranteed solid heads, or oral sex prohibited?

Photo contributed by Brian S. Sheldon

Kuntry Kousins

▼ ▼ ▼ ▼ ▼ ▼ ▼ ▼   ▼ ▼ ▼

Photo contributed by David Marshall

Photos contributed by David Marshall

Photo contributed by Nicole Bassett

. . . and slaw on the side.

MRS. MUSTARD
. . . Allison Pickels

Mustard-Pickels

Allison Leilani Pickels and Charles Stoll Mustard Jr., both of Athens, Ga., were married March 24.

From *The* (Columbia, South Carolina) *State*; contributed by John W. Barrett

Some guys just won't let it go.

Photo contributed by Scott Wingerson

Suicide's not the answer, especially if you have to take the shuttle bus.

Photo contributed by Dr. and Mrs. Wayne V. Miller

Photo contributed by Paul Egan

IF YOU DON'T HAVE A
LAG OR POLE WHY
NOT GET ONE. IN REAR

Photo contributed by Ralph Doty

The parties are fun, but those things really look funny in the refrigerator.

From the *Cleveland Plain Dealer*;
contributed by Eric Ambro

Front-row seats for the three-hanky puppy funeral

Photo contributed by Robert Hatcher

It even reads for you.

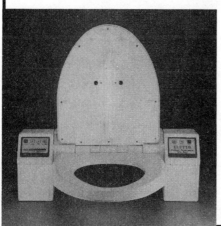

START YOUR DAY WITH **ELETTO**

An Intelligent Toilet Seat

FUNCTIONS:
- Seat Cover Auto Lift-Up
- Seat Cover & Seat Auto Lift-Up
- Temperature Adjusted Seat
- Deodorizing/Air-Freshening Device
- Infrared Ray Detector
- Auto Flushing
- Seat Cover & Seat Auto Lay-Down
- Ultraviolet Sterilization

PATENT

R.O.C.	PAT P76206691
U.S.A.	PAT P98520
ENGLAND	PAT P8723102
W.G.	PAT G8711488.7
JAPAN	PAT P62-150548

From an unidentified magazine;
contributed by Ron Ramsden

Just remove the toilet paper and we'll keep an eye on you.

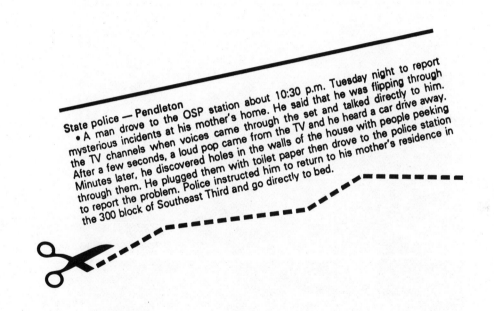

State police — Pendleton
• A man drove to the OSP station about 10:30 p.m. Tuesday night to report mysterious incidents at his mother's home. He said that he was flipping through the TV channels when voices came through the set and talked directly to him. After a few seconds, a loud pop came from the TV and he heard a car drive away. Minutes later, he discovered holes in the walls of the house with people peeking through them. He plugged them with toilet paper then drove to the police station to report the problem. Police instructed him to return to his mother's residence in the 300 block of Southeast Third and go directly to bed.

From the *East Oregonian*;
contributed by Gus Mortier

They hate the hair dryer.

Photo contributed by Hans Tischer, Jr.

Put a gorgeous dame on my chest, and make 'er a spaniel.

Photo contributed by Andy Altschuler

Opie vs. *Death Wish*

OFFICIAL PRIMARY BALLOT
REPUBLICAN PARTY
PASCO COUNTY, FLORIDA
October 2, 1990

STATE		
COMMISSIONER OF AGRICULTURE —Vote for ONE—	**CHARLES BRONSON**	99 →
	RON HOWARD	100 →

Absentee ballot instructions from Pasco County, Florida; contributed by Christina Renke

Sorry. We don't carry it.

Photo contributed by John Goese

Just wipe your shoes before you come in, Phil.

Photo contributed by Thomas H. Bonte

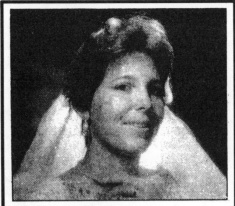

Tamara Long

Long-Moose

HERTFORD, N.C. — Miss Tamara Kay Moose and Mr. Dwayne Andrew Long exchanged vows Saturday, April 8, at 2 p.m. in Holiday Island Park.

From the Virginia Beach *Virginia Pilot/Ledger Star*; contributed by Wendy Woodruff

Headstones for Dead Phonies

Photo contributed by Leon D. Ver Schure

Sesame Spite

Arriving at Hirsch Coliseum March 5 are Sesame Street stars The Cunt, (clockwise from top left) Grover, Big Bird, Cookie Monster, Oscar the Grouch, Prairie Dawn, Ernie and Bert.

From the *Shreveport* (Louisiana) *Times*; contributed by Susan Parmer

And the Bubonic Award goes to . . .

First State Capitol Day Held

Senator Phil Rock, (with plague), being presented the Distinquished Service Award by Ted Scharle, Bradley; Constance Cavany, U of I Urbana; Don Koehn, Illinois Wesleyan; Conley Stutz, Bradley; Art Robinson, U of I Urbana.

From *Illinois Academe*;
contributed by D. S. Knutson

Enduring Problems

Out of the Earth

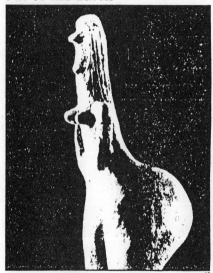

Archeologists recently discovered this figurine at the site of the oldest known farming colony in Europe, near Odzaci, Yugoslavia. Thought to be 7,000 years old, it is 15 inches tall, 10 inches taller than any discovered so far.

Juxtaposed in the Syracuse, New York, *Post-Standard*; contributed by Steven R. King

MINOT
GUN CLUB

ESKIMO SHOOT
APRIL 13-14
COME ONE COME ALL

Photo contributed by Terrence L. Rohrer

You can Pfuhl some of the people some of the time . . .

Photo contributed by David Jackino

Sighting Number 187,308

Photo contributed by Lynn Wiegard

The Next Right

Photo contributed by Steve Stark

Photo contributed by Joyce Palmquist

Photo contributed by Kent Dundee

Humpty's pissed off. Get your own.

Photo contributed by Wayne Leonard

Movie rights, anyone?

Car-bug collision destroys vehicle

The Times-Mail

PAOLI — A Paoli woman miraculously escaped injury when her car flipped after she was blinded when a large bug hit her outside mirror and splattered onto her face and glasses.

The Orange County Sheriff's Department said the 1982 Subaru driven by Peggy Lee, 40, ran off the side of the road and flipped at 11:59 a.m. Lee was four to five miles east of Paoli on U.S. 150. The car was a total loss.

From the Bedford, Indiana, *Times-Mail*; contributed by Bradley Wayne Kalnajs

Conjugal cramp

Sharpe-Payne

Sharpe

Savanna Lynn Payne and Robert Franklin Sharpe III were married July 6 at North Park Presbyterian Church.

The bride is the daughter of Paul R. Payne of Corpus Christi and LaRue Westbrook of Lewisville. The bridegroom is the son of Mr. and Mrs. Robert Franklin Sharpe Jr.

Honor attendants were the bride's mother and the bridegroom's brother, John Kenneth Sharpe of Boulder, Colo.

The couple will live in Austin.

From the *Dallas Morning News*; contributed by Sue McMorris

Photo contributed by Lisa Brandt

Complain and they cry.

Photo contributed by Hans Tischer, Jr.

Don't worry, you won't feel a thing.

Photo contributed by Gina Meyer

What good are they empty?

Public input on condoms sought

Page 3

From the *Edmonton* (Alberta, Canada) *Examiner*;
contributed by David Berger

Emergency Instructions

Photo contributed by Cathy Lander

▼ ▼ ▼ ▼ ▼ ▼ ▼ ▼ ▼ ▼ ▼

Photo contributed by Linda Sherbert

Photo contributed by James M. Ford

Photo contributed by Stephen D. Miller

Flip a coin.

2 Towns Vie For Pizza Hut Sewage

Raritan Township's sewer authority and Flemington are still arguing over which municipality gets to process sewage from an as-yet unbuilt Pizza Hut.

The restaurant has been approved for a vacant tract next to the Flemington Mall that is on the boundary line between the two towns.

According to Gregory Watts, the authority's attorney, the bulk of the property is in Flemington, but the authority has a sewer line that bisects the property and the developer would like to hook into that line.

However, the line then runs through a section of the borough before returning to the township and at no time passes through the Flemington metering station.

The borough planning board has already approved Pizza Hut's request to build. Councilman George Wilson has been insisting that Flemington receive the sewer connection and service charges from the property.

It's the authority view that since sewage from that line wouldn't pass through the borough meter, Flemington wouldn't be charged by the authority. And authority members have said they don't intend to give services away.

At last Wednesday's authority meeting, Watts reiterated the position that since it owns and maintains the line, the authority is entitled to all the fees Pizza Hut would have to pay.

The two groups will meet again to discuss the situation again, but no date has been set.

From the *Hunterdon County* (New Jersey) *Democrat*; contributed by Diana Schwabe

Photo contributed by Dixon Bowles

. . . and a dandelion bouquet, please.

Engagements

Weed, Pickens

Former Fremont resident Mary Kathleen Weed and Samuel David Pickens announced their engagement on Jan. 5 at the home of the bridegroom-elect's parents in Barre, Mass.

They plan to wed on March 20 at the Sisters of the Holy Family Chapel in Mission San Jose. The bride-elect is the daughter of retired U.S. Air Force Lt. Col. and Mrs. Hampton Francis Weed of Fremont. She graduated from Moreau High School in Hayward, the University of California, Davis, and received a Ph.D. from the Sorbonne in Paris. She works for Hewlett-Packard in Geneva, Switzerland.

The bridegroom-elect is the son of Dr. and Mrs. Samuel Claude Pickens of Barre, Mass.

He is a guaduate of Quabbin High School in Barre and Boston University.

He is Editor-in-Chief of "Contact," for Nakia Consumer Electronics in Geneva.

From the *San Francisco Examiner*;
contributed by Dana Hernandez

. . . and you've got the place all to yourselves.

Photo contributed by Philip A. Wood

. . . then take your flasher and get out of here.

Photo contributed by Jerry Mauldin

Photo contributed by Don Liverani

. . . from whence comes the saying "Dead as a dudu."

Photo contributed by R. B. Martin

Think small.

SAFEWAY COUPON

Coupon Good thru 10/14/86

Kellogg's Raisin Brain

20-Oz. Cereal

First 1 With Coupon **$1 99**

One Coupon Per Family/Ptld Division

Save Up To 76¢

BACK·TO·SCHOOL·BACK·TO·SCHOOL·BACK·TO·SCHOOL·T

4459

RAISIN BRAN

Coupon contributed by Joel Ryan Boline

Equal Opportunity Employers

Photo contributed by Margaret Jarvie

Photo contributed by Fran Guyott, Jr.

Shit saves thief

By Lucas Lukumbo of *Shihata*

A SUSPECTED thief smeared his body with his own shit to deter arrest, it has been learnt.

The suspect whose name was not immediately known stole a pair of trousers from a resident along Upanga Road in the city and ran towards the Indian Ocean when people spotted him.

An eyewitness Ndugu Denis Magubila told *Shihata* that the thief was caught at the Gymkhana Golf grounds and was forced to untire the trouser he had already worn inside his worn-out trouser.

Ndugu Magubila said that the thief who seemed to respond the demands of the people to untire the trouser 'kept silent for some minutes forcing himself to shit, and took the shit with his hands and smeared himself with it leaving the people dump-founded.

Nobody could arrest the already smelling middle-aged thief who ran towards the Indian Ocean shore apparently to take a bath.

From the *Daily News* of Dar Es Salaam, Tanzania; contributed by Thomas Hettel

Coming soon: Pavarotti Pantyhose.

Tonight 8:00

Programs you count on— count on you!

8
KAET
Part of
Arizona State University

PASSION, POLITICS AND PAVAROTTI!

Long regarded as a supreme Italian opera, this new production of Giuseppe Verdi's great love poem casts Luciano Pavarotti in a tale of political intrigue, murder and passionate love!

A Masked Ball from the Metropolitan Opera - NEW!

SPIDER VEINS?

"If Your Legs Are Not Becoming To You... You Should Be Coming To Us!!"

A SIMPLE IN OFFICE PROCEDURE WITH NO SURGERY, NO TIME LOSS FROM WORK AND NO UNSIGHTLY SCARS CAN MAKE THOSE VEINS DISAPPEAR.   *Financing Available*

991-0300
SCOTTSDALE INSTITUTE FOR COSMETIC DERMATOLOGY, LTD.

10603 N. Hayden Road, Suite 112

Juxtaposed ads in the *Arizona Republic*;
contributed by Wayne P. Barnard

Vanquish them until they learn.

Photo contributed by Tom Dorman

Colon accused of shoplifting condoms

From the *Columbia* (Missouri) *Daily Tribune*; contributed by Chuck Lay

Boner big winner in women's city

From the *Elkhart* (Indiana) *Truth*; contributed by Chris Edwards

Pull up to the pump and chow down.

▼ ▼ ▼ ▼ ▼ ▼ ▼ ▼ ▼ ▼ ▼ ▼ ▼ ▼ ▼ ▼

Photo contributed by Niles Chandler

Photo contributed by Corey Moyerson

Why's there a line down at Tyson's?

TYSON
BERRYVILLE

Tyson announces a new part-time "FUX" employment program. Anyone interested in earning extra income and having the flexibility of choosing your own work days, is encouraged to apply in person.

From the *Eureka Springs* (Arkansas) *Times-Echo*; contributed by Randy Freeman

The Pride of the Swiss

Photo contributed by Ivor Jones

Move over, Kaopectate.

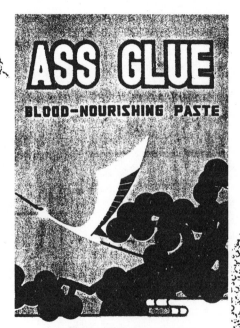

ASS GLUE

BLOOD-NOURISHING PASTE

HUHOHOUT DRUG MANUFACTORY

Huhohout. China

Elixir from China;
contributed by Ophelia Chong

You're getting very sleepy, your honor . . . now repeat after me:
"I find for the plaintiff . . ."

Coupon contributed by C. A. Woody

Funeral Menu

MARY PIZZA

Mary Pizza of Hudson died Sunday at her sister's home in Greenport.

She was born in Italy.

Survivors include her husband, Harry Pizza of Hudson; three sons, Anthony of Binghamton,

HOWARD TOPPING

Howard J. Topping, 73, of Wynantskill, father of Jonnie Davis of North Chatham and Pamela L. Topping of Valatie, died Monday at St. Peter's Hospital, Albany.

Born in Troy, he lived there and

Side-by-side obituaries in the *Independent*; contributed by R. Kane

Photo contributed by Al Theis

Wetter than those other brands!

Photo contributed by George A. Smith

Ohio flood toll rises to 15; dozens missing

SHADYSIDE, Ohio (AP) — Searchers recovered the bodies of four people Saturday, bringing to 15 the confirmed death toll from a flash flood that raged through eastern Ohio, authorities said. About three dozen people remained missing.

A 5-year-old Glencoe girl, Tiffany Webb, was found dead in McMahon Creek early Saturday, said Chuck Vogt, Belmont County coroner's investigator. The girl and her 6-year-old brother, Donald Andrew Webb, were killed when Thursday night's flood swept their mobile home from its concrete mooring.

Later in the day, Vogt reported two additional victims, Danny Humphrey, 8, hometown unknown, and Mary Grimes, age and hometown unknown. A fourth victim, who was not identified, was discovered in the Ohio River late in the afternoon, Vogt said last night.

Capt. Jim Boling of the Ohio Air National Guard said the number of people missing was revised Saturday evening to 34. Previous reports from Belmont County authorities had given the number as 51.

New water manager getting his feet wet

By Thom Akeman
Herald Staff Writer

Jim Cofer has been getting his feet wet for a month now, wading through the problems of the Monterey Peninsula Water Man-

(Herald photo)

JIM COFER

agement District.

So far, he said, he's decided that he needs to set priorities so he doesn't get bogged down.

"I'm trying not to get too sidetracked on rationing and all these interim problems. They could overwhelm us," Cofer said during an interview. "I want to make sure we set our priorities and keep them straight."

The new general manager of the water district said his basic goal will be to enlarge the water supply on the Monterey Peninsula.

He said he is now working his way through the massive environmental impact report for water allocation on the Peninsula and trying to figure out the status of the EIR for a possible dam on the Carmel River.

And as soon as he gets around to it, there are 15 cartons waiting in the corner of his new office, cartons filled with files that former manager Bruce Buel left behind for him to read.

"There's more than I anticipated," Cofer said. "I'm clearly
(Continued on page 4A)

Side-by-side articles in the Monterey, California, *Morning Herald*; contributed by Marci Padfield

... and he'll damned well do what he's told.

Hachette Names Pecker To Run U.S. Magazines

By a WALL STREET JOURNAL Staff Reporter

NEW YORK—Hachette S.A., putting its U.S. magazine operations under the control of an American executive for the first time, named David J. Pecker executive vice president/publishing of the Paris-based media giant's Hachette Magazines Inc. unit.

From the *Wall Street Journal;* contributed by Christopher Chaloux

... while feet head for county line.

Hand waves goodbye to county board

By Ed Tagliaferri
Staff Writer

John Hand, whose low-key leadership helped tame a sometimes volatile Westchester County Board of Legislators, will not run for re-election in November.

Hand, the board's chairman since January 1990 and a legislator for 18 years, said yesterday in a written statement that he would not seek a 10th term so as to "make way for a new generation of leaders who will take our county into the next century."

John Hand

"Ecclesiastes tells us that there is a time for everything. Well, this is the time for John Hand to step down," he said.

From the Westchester County, New York, *Citizen-Register;* contributed anonymously

... with special emphasis on turnips.

Brent Turnipseed

SDSU Adds to Staff

BROOKINGS — South Dakota State University has added two new staff members.

Brent Turnipseed has been named director of the SDSU Seed Lab. He is a native of Minnesota and is finishing his Ph.D. at Mississippi State University. He will also be teaching and leading seed research activities.

From a South Dakota newspaper;
contributed by Kim Korth

Drive with care, caution, concern, concentration, and courage.

Photo contributed by Carl O. Kaufmann

WE FEAST YOUR TASTE RIGHT ROYALLY

✿

KERALA

TANDOORI

CHINESE

PUNJABI

CONTINENTAL
and what have you.,
walk in to our-
roof garden and
fall on top of the
world.

Photo contributed by Leo Buccellato

Johnson - Wax

Vows of marriage will be spoken on April 20, 1991, by Michelle Lee Johnson and David John Wax, both of Creek Drive, Kentwood.

The bride-to-be is the daughter of Sue Johnson of Lake Odessa and Gerald Johnson of Hastings.

From the *Hastings* (Michigan) *Reminder*; contributed by Kim Eldred

. . . and don't stop for gas either.

By-Pass Restaurant

Photo contributed by Paul Ellis

From the Instant Soup Department

Sales materials for a laboratory supply firm;
contributed by Graham Wren

And what a swell team it must be.

Photo contributed by Gail Folda

. . . for it leaves tire tracks on the sunbathers.

Photo contributed by Linda Ontko Welp

Body search reveals $4,000 in crack

From the *Jackson* (Michigan) *Citizen-Patriot*;
contributed by Tom Oswald

MISSI G, Part II

▼ ▼ ▼ ▼ ▼ ▼ ▼ ▼ ▼ ▼ ▼

Photo contributed by Brian Carter

Photo contributed by Stacy Fisher

Photo contributed by Beth Kuebler

Photo contributed by Jack Kunces

And now for the local news . . .

Personnel at the Farmers First Bank on N. Cedar Street reported at 10:15 a.m. on May 13 the discovery of a mound of hair on May 10,

From the police log section of the Lancaster, Pennsylvania, *Intelligencer Journal*; contributed by Brian K. Snavely

Potato assault
An 18-year-old man was charged with fourth-degree assault Saturday. According to Alaska State Troopers, Jacob Mears of North Pole was arrested shortly after 7 p.m. for throwing a potato at his mother.

From the *Fairbanks Daily News-Miner*; contributed by Fred Wilkins

April 20
12:29 p.m. a young man at 207 West Fifth reported that someone had taken his car radio out of his vehicle, placed it in the street and had driven over it several times.

From the *Gordon* (Nebraska) *Journal*; contributed by Tracy B. Baker

Beaver—Trimmer

NEW OXFORD — St. Paul's "The Pines" Lutheran Church was the setting for the Dec. 15 wedding of Janet L. Beaver and Gary R. Trimmer. The Rev. B. Tim Wagner performed the double ring ceremony at 5 p.m.

A resident of 303 N. Bolton St., the bride is the daughter of Charles and Ann Beaver, Northumberland RD1. The bridegroom is the son of Edwin and Romaine Trimmer, 2147 Hunterstown/Hampton Road, New Chester.

Given in marriage by her father, the bride wore a pale pink wedding gown of satin. It was styled with a natural waistline, and the satin bodice featured a shirred center panel of re-embroidered lace with sequins and pearl drops. The long, satin sleeves had a double shoulder puff which extended into a fitted sleeve of English net and satin. The back bodice featured a deep V and a butterfly satin bow at the waistline.

The full satin skirt was edged at the hemline with a a scalloped border of re-embroidered lace. The skirt extended into a sweeping cathedral-length train.

Lisa Tomalavage of Dauphin was the matron of honor. Chosen as the bridesmaids were Melissa Frantz and Sandy Kase, both of Northumberland. Brittany Beaver of Northumberland was the flower girl.

Serving as the best man was Willie Musselman of York Springs. The ushers were Jeff Murren and Charles Becker, both of Hanover. Jason Trimmer of Abbottstown and Dustin Beaver of Northumberland were the ring bearers.

Ruth Dellinger of Gettysburg provided the organ music. The vocalists were Marcia Knorr of Hanover and Ted Schott of East Berlin.

A reception for 175 guests followed in Heidlersburg Firehall. The newlyweds are living at 489 Frazer Road, Aspers.

The bride is a 1980 graduate of Shikellamy High School and a 1987 graduate of Bloomsburg University. She is pursuing a master's degree at

Mr. and Mrs. Gary Trimmer

Western Maryland College and is a teacher for Lincoln Intermediate Unit No. 12.

The bridegroom is a 1983 graduate of New Oxford High School and is a carpenter and crew leader for Barry Bechtel General Contractor Inc.

From the Sunbury, Pennsylvania, *Daily Item*; contributed by T. C. Retallack

Bird on a Hook

TURKY'S TOWING

24 hour

TOWING SERVICE

766-9815

P.O. Box 39750 • Charleston, SC 29407

IF YOU NEED A JERK, CALL THE TURK!

Business card contributed by John Smith

It'sa costa lessa uppa the road.

Photo contributed by Scott Morris

Compulsory School—the Case in Favor

Photo contributed by R. J. Swanson

Photo contributed by Paul Nine

It sounds like war in there at lunchtime.

Photo contributed by Ron Ramsden

. . . He was over at Belchers making noise.

Photo contributed by Angus Bromley

Photo contributed by Dierdre Serio

Getting paid for what they do best.

County wants money for taking dump

By Suzanne Gamboa
Associated Press

SIERRA BLANCA, Texas — Hudspeth County should be compensated by the state and Texas utilities for the happened we lost all our negotiating power," he said.

The utilities aren't willing to make any payments until they know the dump's location is permanent.

The state initially proposed building the dump in Fort Hancock, about 60 miles east of Downtown El Paso, and now is studying the area near Sierra Blanca, about 90 miles east of Downtown.

In January, state District

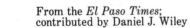

From the *El Paso Times*;
contributed by Daniel J. Wiley

You better get over here, boss. The washers attacked the freezers, and there's Freon all over the place.

Photo contributed by Christina Renke

For Light Sleepers

Photo contributed by Marc Brewer

Eat and die.

Photo contributed by Chad Miller

Cancellation. "God's Trying to Tell You Something," scheduled for 8 tonight in the Civic Center has been canceled. Tickets can be returned to the Civic Center box office or to the place of purchase for a refund.

From the *Des Moines Register*; contributed by Kara L. Gipson

Look but don't squeeze.

Photo contributed by Daniel Barth

Paul — Newman

Jill Ann Newman, daughter of Dr. William and Judie Richman of Hollywood, FL and Rodger and Adele Newman of Akron, OH, has become engaged to Steven G. Paul, D.V.M., son of Norman and Florrie Paul of Boca Raton.

From the *Miami Herald*;
contributed by David Rutman

Roberts-Pinkstaff

Cheryl F. Pinkstaff and Arthur L. Roberts Jr. were married March 9 at Los Altos Methodist Church.

The bride is the daughter of Robert A. Akins Sr., Louisville, Ky., and Sadie M. Moles, Hurricane, W.Va. A graduate of Milpitas High School and San Jose State University, she is a police officer in Newark.

The bridegroom is the son of Arthur L. Roberts Sr. and Ruth A. Roberts, Mountain View.

From the *San Jose Mercury News*;
contributed by Kevin Cronin

Rest Rooms for Customers Only

Compliments of:

WEE · WEE
RESTAURANT & DISCO PUB

M.O.A. RICE & PALAY DEALER
62 RIZAL AVE., LUCBAN, QUEZON
TELEPHONE NO. 217

ARCO SWINE & POULTRY FARM
BO. KULAPI, LUCBAN, QUEZON

JANUARY				1984		
SUN	MON	TUE	WED THU	FRI	SAT
1	2	3	4	5	6	7
8	9	10	11	12	13	14
15	16	17	18	19	20	21
22	23	24	25	26	27	28
29	30	31				

FEBRUARY
1984

MARCH				1984		
SUN	MON	TUE	WED THU	FRI	SAT
					1	2	3
4	5	6	7	8	9	10
11	12	13	14	15	16	17
18	19	20	21	22	23	24
25	26	27	28	29	30	31

From a Filipino calendar;
contributed by Roland Hanewald

Please unwrap cabbage before eating.

Photo contributed by Jeremy Foster

Shades of Justice

BLACK, BLACK & BROWN
ATTORNEYS

Photo contributed by Mark Barra

Beware of purple rain.

Photo contributed by Larry S. Ferguson

Mystery Motor Lodge

Photo contributed by E. A. Minahan

Try plant food.

Police ask for tips
on marijuana growing

LOWVILLE — Lewis County Sheriff's deputies want the community's help to find people who grew marijuana plants in the town of West Turin.

Sixty plants, each about 4 feet tall, were found yesterday in a remote area of the town. The plants were cut down.

People with information should call the department at 376-3511.

From the *Utica* (New York) *Observer-Dispatch*; contributed by Steve Holstein

Shoppers' Choice: Brand-Name Motels

▼ ▼ ▼ ▼ ▼ ▼ ▼ ▼ ▼ ▼ ▼ ▼ ▼ ▼

Photo contributed by Joe Patrick

Photo contributed by Richard Terrill

Photo contributed by Scott Pritchett

Barefoot, Herring Engaged

Ruth Ellen Herring

Ms. Toshiko Higo Herring of Spring Lake announces the engagement of her daughter, Ruth Ellen Herring of Linden, to Eldridge Rudolph Barefoot Jr. of Spring Lake, son of Eldridge Rudolph Barefoot Sr. of Spring Lake.

The wedding will be held on May 4 at Bethel Baptist Church.

From the *Spring Lake* (New Jersey) *News*; contributed by Glenn Riccio

CORRECTIONS

A Thursday story incorrectly quoted Councilman Stewart Clifton as calling Mayor Bill Boner a "squeeze-bag." Clifton called Boner a "sleaze-bag."

From the *Nashville Banner*;
contributed by Mike Long

Photo contributed by Rita Whale

Photo contributed by Andrea McGuire

Beans and a Great Big Exhaust Fan

Photo contributed by Josh and Matt Levine

Mollusk Nerds

THE SMOKEHOUSE

Reg. $2.98 lb.

SMOKED OYSTER DINKS

$2⁴⁹ lb.

From the (Boise) *Idaho Statesman*; contributed by M. Betournay

Pour me another prime rib, Al.

Photo contributed by Marci Ward

And now for the best-groomed couple . . .

Yong Photography

**DIANE and
DENNIS HAYRE**

Hayre-Combs

Diane Amy Combs and Dennis Duraine Hayre chose the First Presbyterian Church as the setting for their May 11 wedding.

From the *Stockton* (California) *Record*; contributed by Pat Jones

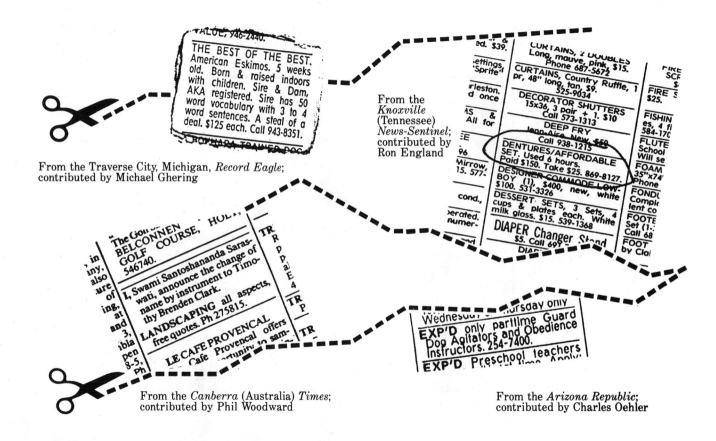

VALUE? 946-2440.

THE BEST OF THE BEST. American Eskimos. 5 weeks old. Born & raised indoors with children. Sire & Dam, AKA registered. Sire has 50 word vocabulary with 3 to 4 word sentences. A steal of a deal. $125 each. Call 943-8351.

From the Traverse City, Michigan, *Record Eagle*; contributed by Michael Ghering

From the *Knoxville* (Tennessee) *News-Sentinel*; contributed by Ron England

DENTURES/AFFORDABLE SET. Used 6 hours. Paid $150. Take $25. 869-8127.

The Goan BELCONNEN GOLF COURSE, HOL 546740.

I, Swami Santoshananda Saraswati, announce the change of name by instrument to Timothy Brenden Clark.

LANDSCAPING all aspects, free quotes. Ph 275815.

LE CAFE PROVENCAL Cafe Provencal offers

From the *Canberra* (Australia) *Times*; contributed by Phil Woodward

Wednesday, Thursday only

EXP'D only parttime Guard Dog Agitators and Obedience Instructors. 254-7400.

EXP'D Preschool teachers

From the *Arizona Republic*; contributed by Charles Oehler

We're practically giving them away!

Photo contributed by David Edwards

No, dear, I don't think a cat fancier's parking lot would be full of four-by-fours, pickups, and semis.

Photo contributed by Carl Salas

A present for the ex?

Photo contributed by Dan Felter

Tickles would have wanted it this way.

Photo contributed by Russ Meyer

Photo contributed by George Mickelson

NU female faculty eyed by senators

From The Associated Press

The University of Nebraska must
ke spec _ _ _ ediate action to
_ _ _ ng, promotion
_ _ v and staff
_ _ unty legis-

From the *Lincoln* (Nebraska) *Journal-Star*;
contributed by Tom Ulrich

He wasn't in the mood.

Cops Kill Music Fan

Jacksonville, Fla.

Police responding to com-
plaints that Ronald Neil Boyd, 56,
was playing Glenn Miller music too
loud killed him in an exchange of
gunfire that they say he started.

Associated Press

From the *San Francisco Chronicle*;
contributed by Marty Stuzinski

. . . and a wedge of Muenster to hang over the fireplace.

Photo contributed by David Deeds

Toward Greater Consumer Confidence

▼ ▼ ▼ ▼ ▼ ▼ ▼ ▼ ▼ ▼ ▼ ▼ ▼ ▼ ▼ ▼ ▼

Photo from unidentified magazine; contributed by Sean Swidnicki

Photo contributed by David W. Wilhelm

Photo contributed by David Kovl

Sack the minister.

engaged

Lawrence - Taylor

KERHONKSON — Mrs. Vena Quick announces the engagement of her daughter, Chesty Stacia Lawrence, to Tracy Michael Taylor, son of Mr. and Mrs. Victor M. Taylor, Rosendale. Miss Lawrence is also the daughter of the late Edward William Lawrence.

The future bride is a graduate of Kingston High School and BOCES. She is employed at Mohonk Mountain House, New Paltz.

Her fiance attended Rondout Valley High School. He is a self-employed carpenter.

A wedding in June is planned.

From the Middletown, New York, *Times Herald Record*; contributed by Richard Roda

Slogan or confession?

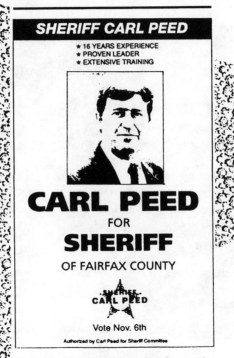

SHERIFF CARL PEED

★ 16 YEARS EXPERIENCE
★ PROVEN LEADER
★ EXTENSIVE TRAINING

CARL PEED
FOR
SHERIFF
OF FAIRFAX COUNTY

SHERIFF
CARL PEED

Vote Nov. 6th

Authorized by Carl Peed for Sheriff Committee

From the *Fairfax* (Virginia) *Connection;*
contributed by Charles Winkler

So where is . . . THE MERCHANDISE?

Photo contributed by Peter Lorenz

. . . not on you, we hope.

Photo contributed by Floyd Gellerman

Wrinkled minnows and bible-pressed worms.

Photo contributed by Ed Thornburg

. . . where the ambulance squad drowned doing mouth-to-mouth.

Photo contributed by Randy Bender

Captivating container or passionate pugilism?

Photo contributed by David Thrower

C.K. HAIR-RESTORATION
GIVES ME A NEW LOOK

I sing like Elvis Presley. But my
balding head didn't look like him!
So I came to CK Hair Centre for a
hair restoration programme. Now I
can take shower, swim and sing as
if I had my real hair back. CK
helps restore my
style. Not even my
girlfriends know
the secret.

Gary Jung — The
new Elvis Presley

C.K. Hair Centre
15/F, Sanwa Bldg., 30-32 Connaught Rd. C.
5-258861

✂

To: C.K. Hair Centre
15th Floor, Sanwa Bldg.,
30-32 Connaught Rd., H.K.

Please send me details
of the C.K. Hair-Restoration Technique.

Name:_____
Age:_____
Address:_____
_____
_____
Occupation:_____
Tel:_____

From the Hong Kong
South China Morning Post;
contributed by Kevin Fellman

Overtime Nuptials

LONG-DAY

Lisa Denise Day and Douglas Anthony Long were married April 6 at Rivercliff Lutheran Church in Roswell.

The bride is the daughter of Priscilla Edwards of Lexington, S.C., and Dr. Richard R. Day of Rome, Ga. She is a graduate of the University of Georgia and is employed by E.T. Booth Middle School.

The bridegroom is the son of Lucretia Davies of Savannah and Thomas E. Long Jr. of Green Cove Springs, Fla. He is a graduate of Virginia Commonwealth University and is employed by Dean Rusk Middle School in Canton.

After a cruise to the Caribbean, the couple will live in Woodstock.

From *The Atlanta Journal-Constitution*; contributed by Chuck Buell

Where all medical options are exhausted.

Photo contributed by Steve Makela

Seafood Malaise

Photo contributed by Christopher M. Landrum

Photo contributed by Christopher M. Landrum

Photo contributed by Rick Kestenbaum

Snacks and Semiautomatics

All Gunsmithing

STOP BY
Rifles, Shotguns
& Handguns

BUY,
SELL,
TRADE,
CONSIGNMENTS
WELCOME
REFERENCES

GIRL SCOUT COOKIES
W/EACH GUN PURCHASED

MONTANA GUN WORKS
Smith&Wesson SERVICE CENTER
3017 10TH AVE. S. • GREAT FALLS • 761-4346

From *Consumers Press* of Montana;
contributed by Dave Farley

Love and Plagiarism

personal ads.
333-3662. FREE!

Scott, Just hearing your name, makes me smile, your beauty makes me short of breath, I pray that one day, you will say, I Love You, J.B. as much as I love you right now and I mean this with all my heart. I Love You, Baby. J.B.★★★P.S., I'm not going too fast, this is just me.

TERI, Just hearing your name makes me smile, your beauty makes me short of breath, I pray that one day you will say I Love You Scott as much as I love you right now. And I mean this w/all my heart. I Love You Baby, Scott.. P.S. I'm not going too fast, this is just me.

From the *Dallas Times-Herald*;
contributed by Paul Martin

. . . and a bib for Lobo, please.

Wolfe-Spittle

Barbara Ann Wolfe of Oak View and John Spittle of Ventura are announcing their engagement and plan to be married on June 1 at the First Christian Church in Ventura.

The bride-to-be, daughter of Bernie and Shirley Wolfe of Oak View, is a 1986 graduate of Ventura High School. She is an order clerk for Paradise Chevrolet.

The prospective groom, son of Bob and Gloria Spittle of Ventura, is a 1984 graduate of Ventura High School. He is an auto mechanic for Paradise Chevrolet.

From the *Ventura County* (California) *Star Free Press*; contributed by Tom McDonnell

When you want the job done right . . .

Photo contributed by James Stinson

The Case for a Lawn Service

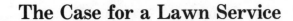

Wife says Weeding killed her husband

From the *San Diego Union*;
contributed by Jim Hopkins

Fun for People Who Spit When They Talk

Photo contributed by Wendy Viets

Try Our Famous Chico Chops

Photo contributed by Jerry Kehn

. . . as witnessed by your local notority public.

The Eighties:
Decade Of Notority

From the Stuart, Virginia, *Bull Mountain Bugle*;
contributed by Beverly Dillard

Bathing suits and Band-Aids required.

Photo contributed by Viki Bankey

Self-Multiplying Automobile

Photo contributed by Max Apeture

Freshly Squeezed

Photo contributed by Richard Deight

the Carroll-
anch   area.
ork indepen-
    as a team
ted, please
838 between
day through

(10 hours week). Part...
level required. Send resume to:
...N.... E......way.
Suite 209, Dallas, Texas 75206.

WANTED: Back End Assistant
for 1 doctor gynecologist office. Very near Richardson
Medical Center. Good hours.
Light lab. Health insurance
paid. Experience desired. In-
quire @ ███ aft 5 P.M.

RN/LVN
Exciting position for flexible
person with endocrine prac-
tice, Mon-Fri. Presbyterian
area. Non-smoker. Call for interview, ███

OMIST

RN needed to work
Internal...

...logist
s area. Full
e. Must be
ire MTASCP
least 1 year
erience and a
nse, car pro-
erview 1-800-
-S. Bring re-
ces.

orthopedic
resume to
Lemmon Av

Medical Re
Experienced
rollton. Plea
795601, Dalla
ME
Apply in pe
1040 E. N.V
48-1490.

Analytical
dent contra
Pam Lancar

Nurse part-
Non-smoker
Walter Reec
PEDIAT

From the *Dallas Morning News*;
contributed by Larry Brautigam

The Good Book and a Can of Lysol

Photo contributed by Paddy O'Leary

A.k.a. Frankfurter

LONG/HAMBURGER

Julie A. Long and Michael J. Hamburger were joined in marriage Sept. 9 at Congregation Neveh Shalom. The bridegroom wore his father's ring for the ceremony. Maui, Hawaii, was their honeymoon destination.

The bride, a self-employed hairdresser, is the daughter of Gena K. Long of Forest Grove. The bridegroom, a national sales manager, is graduate of the University of Oregon. Inga Hamburger of Lake Oswego is his mother.

From *The Oregonian*; contributed by Richard H. Kingsley

... featuring the famous three-foot sausage!

Photo contributed by Edward G. Kosco

Caution: Allow ample time to lower lifeboats when scheduling emergencies.

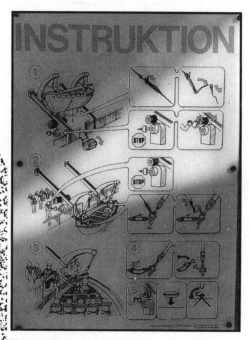

Photo contributed by Richard L. Turner

. . . and Pat takes in laundry.

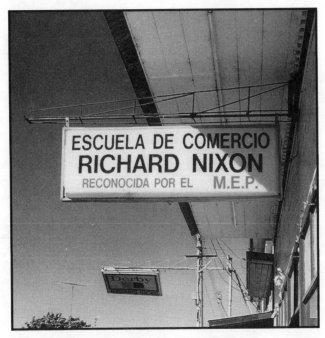

Photo contributed by Steven M. Krauzer

The Last Honest Man

♦ ♦ ♦ ♦ ♦ ♦ ♦ ♦ ♦ ♦ ♦ ♦ ♦ ♦ ♦ ♦ ♦

SITUATIONS WANTED

♦ ♦ ♦ ♦ ♦ ♦ ♦ ♦ ♦ ♦ ♦ ♦ ♦ ♦ ♦ ♦ ♦

PROFESSIONAL FAILURE

seeks position; This is
NO JOKE! Harvard grad,
sales/mktg background.
Incredible hard luck &
jinx power defy logic
& reason; everything I
touch crumbles. I can
blight businesses, in-
vestments, & industry.
Over 10 yrs. exp. If U
have a LEGITIMATE use
for these abilities,
please reply in confi-
dence.

From the *Boston Globe*;
contributed by Michael C. Michalczyk

You can't even pitch a tent on it.

Photo contributed by Mike Gonzalez

Wildlife Washers

▼ ▼ ▼ ▼ ▼ ▼ ▼ ▼   ▼ ▼ ▼ ▼ ▼

Photo contributed by Bonni Backe

Photo contributed by Ken Koshiol

Photo contributed by Christopher A. Foster

Sand 'er down and she'll be just as good as new.

Fuller-Bumps

CHINA — Heidi Jo Bumps and Dean Edward Fuller were married Oct. 13 at the Baptist Church. A reception followed at the Winslow VFW. The bride is the daughter of Arulde and Christa Bumps. The bridegroom is the son of Guy and Ruth Fuller of Palermo.

The maid of honor was Wendy Nelson of Albion. Bridesmaids were Gloria Keay, Noel Martin and Susie Nelson, all of Albion, and Tiffany Bona of Waterville.

The best man was Jerry Fuller of Palermo. Ushers were Daryl Keay, Ricky Nelson and Rusty Nelson, all of Albion, and Trevy Bumps.

The bride, a graduate of Erskine Academy, is employed by LaVerdiere's Super Drug Stores' main office. Her husband, also a graduate of Erskine Academy, is employed by R&D Masonry.

The couple resides in Albion.

Mr. and Mrs. Dean E. Fuller
(Heidi Jo Bumps)

From the (Waterville) *Central Maine Morning Sentinel*; contributed by R. E. Nelson

Delivering Salvation

Photo contributed by Gregory Doria

We'll troubleshoot your bison.

Photo contributed by Edward G. Kosco

After sushi burgers, dessert.

Photo contributed by Lori and Bob Butler

The astronauts complained it's clammy in there.

NOTICE

LAUNCHING OF SALAMA CONDOM

We wish to inform our esteemed invitees for the function of launching the

SALAMA CONDOM

scheduled for 12th June, 1991 at The Kilimanjaro Hotel, that it has been postponed due to an unavoidable circumstances.

We regret for any inconveniences that might have been caused.

PHARMAPLAST (T) LIMITED.

90235/155906

From the *Daily News* of Dar Es Salaam, Tanzania; contributed by Chris Mawdsley

OWH'S ACUPUNCTURE

TEL· 460-4026

Photo contributed by Ray Sanow

We grow 'em big, growly, and greasy.

Photo contributed by Allan A. Miller

Photo contributed by Louis Angelwolf

Photo contributed by Damon Foster

If you enjoyed **National Lampoon Presents More True Facts**, try the first book from Contemporary, **National Lampoon Presents True Facts**, available in your local bookstore or by mail. To order directly, return the coupon below with payment to: Contemporary Books, Customer Service Department, 180 North Michigan Avenue, Chicago, Illinois 60601. Or call (312) 782-9181 to order with your credit card.

Qty.	Title/Author	Price	Total
____	National Lampoon Presents True Facts (4006-8)	$7.95 ea.	$_____
	Add $1.50 postage for the first book ordered.		$__1.50__
	Add $.75 postage for each additional book ordered.		$_____
	Illinois residents add 7% sales tax; California residents add 6% sales tax.		$_____
	□ Enclosed is my check/money order payable to Contemporary Books.	**Total Price**	$_____

Bill my □ VISA ⎫ Account No. _____ Expiration Date _____
    □ MasterCard ⎭ Signature _____

Name _____

Address _____

City/State/Zip _____

For quantity discount information, please call the sales department at (312) 782-9181. Allow four to six weeks for delivery. *Offer expires March 31, 1993.*

NL391